Dedicated to all the radical romantics and healing hearts who never lost their lust for wander.

Mad Love | Volume 1

LOVE 7

BLISS 39

LUST 63

MELANCHOLY 85

A note from my heart

I love these sage words by Leonard Cohen, "Poetry is just the evidence of life. If your life is burning well, poetry is just the ash."

I've always wanted to be a writer. So I've always written poetry, prose, musings, and messy journal scribbles, quietly imagining that I'd publish my words one day in hopes that they would resonate with someone just as other people's published work has spoken to me – moved me.

Even saved me.

But I'm not here to save anyone. Instead, I'm here to share, to be open, and to create. I'm here to grow, reflect, and heal.

I'm here to be human. I'm here fulfilling my dream of becoming a writer.

Of revealing the poet, I know that I am.

Whether you picked up this anthology to support me, to read, or just out of curiosity – my creative spirit thanks you. I thank you.

This collection of prose is extracted from my journals from around 2010 and a few years after that – my Melbourne years – a chapter in my life when I moved down under to fall in love with a boy, but I ended up falling in love with myself instead. It was a beautiful and heartbreaking adventure. And one of the best chapters of my life.

"Mad love" is a mantra, valediction, and complimentary close that my younger self used to show affection. I'm keeping it in vogue as I age because I couldn't think of a better way to express my deep gratitude and admiration for writing, nature, community, strangers, friends, family, and lovers.

Mad love,
Nicxo

April 2, 2024
Cobourg, Ontario, Canada

LOVE

LOST LOVE

You've always been there.
Lingering at the back of my heart.
You will always be there.

I don't think about you often
But when I do
It's a profound, enduring lust.
I don't yearn for you
Like I used to.
I'm happy now.
I'm with the love of my life –
The love for the rest of my life.

Yet I'm fond of you.
Fond of our chapter
Our romance
But more importantly
Fond of our friendship.
You gave me courage
Heartbreak and redemption
In less than a dozen kisses.

Meeting you was in light years.
A figment of my imagination
That somehow came true.
Even though you've become a stranger
You'll always be one of
My most favourite encounters.

MELBOURNE

She fell in love
With a place
Not a person
Her name was Melbourne

Gritty and arty
Industrial and illuminating
Her hidden laneways
Painted in graffiti
Cluttered with terrace houses
Old pubs and opt shops
HIpster cafes and culinary legends
Speakeasies and spoken word spaces
North and south
Separated by a river
Paths that connected people
To water and green spaces
A city both moody and marvelous
It was love at first sight
A near four year affair
A curious tryst
A turbulent adventure
Where her truest self
Was found

She fell in love
With a place
Not a person
Her name was Melbourne

STANDING STILL

"I will love you even when time doesn't standstill."
He said to her,
But she kept spinning.

THANK YOU FOR THE DANCE

All is gone
But she hasn't forgotten
The day she felt
When they first met.

Two lovers
In a dangerous time
Wild hearts, intertwined.

Their fervor love
Lit up the night
Like crashing thunder
Burning bright.

Until their season
Of sweet passion
And slow romance
Came to an unequivocal end

When she whispered
"Goodbye, my love.
Thank you for the dance."

LOVE IN ALL THE WAYS

I have loved you in all the ways:
The right ways
The wrong ways
The you-don't-deserve-me ways.

HAUNTED LOVE

Our love was the unrequited kind
Yet in some magnificent
Melancholic way
The ghost of you remains
And your shadow lingers
As you continue to haunt
My unbroken, benevolent heart.

MY POST-IT NOTE

Dear Man of Mine,

*I loved you honestly and wholeheartedly
for the longest time.*

*Now, in recent memory,
you are the furthest thing from my mind.*

My head and heart are mine again.

*Mad love,
The girl you never deserved xo*

YOU AND ME, SCARED

That first night we kissed
You said you were scared
Not at all prepared.

So, this is what I propose we do.

In return for your nervous trust,
I will use my words to tell my love for you
And I will ease your fears with the joy of me and you.

You and me
Scared
More than a million works of art
The curators of a great love story
The writers of a one hit wonder.

IF ALL WE HAVE IS TODAY

And if tomorrow never comes
I would be okay
For I was to spend some of my best days
With you
Yesteryear wrapped up
In a lifetime
With the one that I loved

LOVE IN BLOOM

At dusk
When the stars kissed the night
You and me
There under the blankets
Felt so right
As I woke to birdsongs
Cascaded in morning light
My young love for you
Began to ignite

A MUSEUM OF YOU

My mind is a museum of you
Archived remnants of romance
Vintage polaroid memories
On display for only me to see

My mind is an exhibit of you
Filled with portraits of you and I
A rare collection of artifacts
Preserved for the rest of time

My mind is a museum of you
A rare work of art
Perfectly imprinted
Deeply within my heart

YOU DIDN'T HAVE TO LEAVE

When I miss you
It is fully and completely
The way you taste
After breakfast in bed
That last sweet kiss
On my bare forehead
And although I don't
Think about you much
I wish you were still here
With your naked hands
And sweet, tender touch

A LOVE LIKE HEMINGWAY

A piece of you
Is a part of me
But as Hemingway mused
My love for you
Is an unidentified something
That you lost
And the whole of me
Is what I found
Once you were gone

LAY YOUR WORDS

Lay your words down on me
Lay your love into me
Lay your fears in front of me
Lay your joys inside of me

Lay beside me
And love me
For a lifetime or more

UNTIL WE GO

Say your words
Feel your love
Face your fears
Revel in your joys
Lean on me
Even in darkness
Stay with me
Until we let go
And become free

(un)REGRETTED LOVE

My love waits for you
It yearns for you
But my hearts stops
It beats on
My pulse for you
Regrettably gone

WHEN I MET YOU

I loved you for all the minutes before I even knew you.
I started to forget you the moment I met you.

LONG DISTANCE LOVER

Dear long-distance lover,
I wish you were here
Or me there
With you.

COORDINATES

Adventure comes not from what you're discovering
But from whom you're discovering it with.
So get lost.
Fall in love.
Break hearts.
Mend your broken one.
Make memories with strangers
The ones that become lovers
And the ones that become regrets.
Love is an adventure.
Your heart is the map.
Grab a compass, head north.
There's no need to look back.

WHEN WORDS DON'T MATTER

The greater the silence
The sweeter the dance.
The less unknown
The better the sex.

WILL YOU STILL LOVE ME, TOMORROW

If I were to say *"I love you"*
And then you let me go
I would still endure every sorrow
Simply just to know
If you'll love me tomorrow.

GOODBYE

"It is time to leave one another."
She said to him through tears.
*"But let's not say goodbye
In the hope we meet again."*

He took her hand and kissed it.
As he got up to leave, he whispered,

*"I'll see you soon sweet girl.
Either in conversation or prose.
I'll look for you when you're wandering
Down the lonely open road."*

A HEART PASSPORT

To love once is not much of an adventure.
But to love deeply and differently
Now that's an around the world trip.
A heart passport filled with memories
And postcards with no return address.
Love is a vagabond
And like a boomerang
True love always has a way
Of finding its way back home.

STRANGERS

I never truly knew
Just how beautiful a stranger was ...

Until I met you.

BETRAYAL

Your love for her
Is pure bliss
You told me so
When you sealed it
With a kiss

YOUNG LOVE

Even though she adored him very much
Hers was a young love
That never really grew up.

Young hearts break up
Because they think they are growing old
When really, it's the mind coming of age.
For not every enduring relationship
Is forever after.
Even though they once believed
They were soulmates.

5 A.M.

The sun is rising
It's 5 a.m.
They had been talking
And crying
All through the night
But as the day braked
So too did her heart
As he looked at her and spoke
"I will love you like no other
But it is time for me to go."
And so, he did
Leaving her to mourn
A love that left her
Sitting in the dark

WHISKEY & LOVE

When friends become lovers – she wrote a note to herself on a whiskey stained napkin:

Be still my heart
Be calm in my mind
For when I first met you
No love could I find
But then in that moment
With your enduring first kiss
I knew if you stopped
You would be eternally missed

GONE

You're the favourite part of my life story
Even if you're not a part of it anymore.

YOU WERE MY FAVOURITE SEASON

A winter's sleep
Is lonely without your autumn kiss
That last day of summer
When you said I would be missed
In spring I thought I saw you
But the seasons whirled around me
And in bed with the rain
The snow always made me lonely too

BLISS

FRACTURED LIGHT

"There is a crack in everything," Leonard sang.
"That's how the light gets in."

Fractured rays of glowing luminescence
Burns through her splintered heart.
Broken shards and tattered wounds
Of a soul taking risk to explore
A love that enamored her from the start..

"There is a reason for everything," she wrote.
"That's how life gets lived."

HERE - WHERE YOU NEED TO BE

Find peace sweet darling
Calm your frantic heart
Life is as curious
As it is chaotic
Emotions are fleeting
And memories will fade
But you are here
Exactly where you need to be

SERENDIPITY

In your hands
I am home.
I am seen.
I am known.
For all my wandering
With you I roam
Each day together
In harmonic bliss
Our forever after
Fated by a young
Serendipitous kiss.

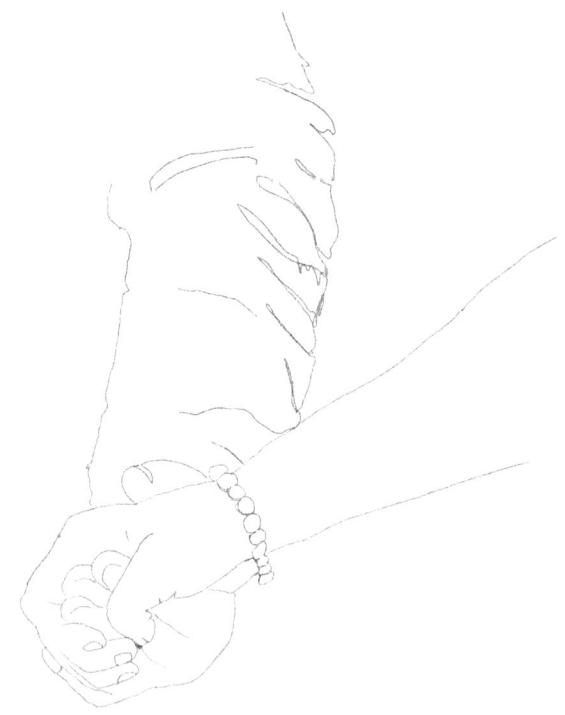

ME & I

Me and I
We go good together.
Two fools
Sharing one heart
The same soul
Intertwined forever
For an eternity of mad love.

FOREIGN FEELINGS

A wandering mind
That takes thoughts to
Curious spaces
A beating heart,
That takes feelings
To foreign places

DIRECTIONS

You go this way
And I'll go that way
No matter where we end up
I promise you
We will meet
Somewhere again
Along the way
And when we do
Our broken hearts
Will have mend

PRESENCE

In those fleeting moments
When nostalgia overwhelms you
Be still - breathe.
Look at the beautiful happenings around you
Embrace the many memories-in-the-making
Being made right in front of you.

Be here today sweet friend
For tomorrow always comes too soon.

BEDLAM & BEAUTY

Life is a beautiful calamity.
It's the messes that we learn the most from.
The imperfections that make us flawless.
And those little innocent failures that make us strong believers
That this life of bedlam and craze
Is worth living.

BIRD'S NEST

Look forward
Not back.
You will see so much more.
Of the world when you walk it
Traverse the scenic route.
Find your own way around
And should you get lost?
Explore it.
For your heart will grow
From an offroad adventure.

FLY

You can always go backwards in life
It is moving forward
That won't happen
While you are standing still

THE POSTCARD

The sound of a postcard is a pretty thing.
So, write letters
To old friends
Unrequited lovers
Strangers you will never meet.
Use a stamp or leave it behind.
For someone else's reading pleasure
Postcards provide enduring romance.
Put a smile on someone's face!
When they open the door
And realize to their surprise
That they've got mail.

COLLISION

Turning ambivalence into beauty
Is what you do
Making commotion out of chaos
Is what I do
Together
Collided
We are the quintessential two.

JOHNNY & DOLLY

Johnny Cash cool
And Dolly Parton pretty
Country music is when
Her heart
First started dreaming

GROWING UP

From naivety and confusion
To a humble confidence
Only endearing for oneself.
Returning to those that knew her
When she was young
To show them the woman
She has proudly become.
But she will leave again
For her spirit she's still exploring
Her character she's still shaping
Her life she's still living.

PRETTY THINGS

Sweet butterfly kisses
Soft bluebird wings
A mad crazy world
Filled with such pretty things.

WHEN A PIXIE LOVES A GNOME

Said the gnome to the pixie:
"Your fairy tale is hiding somewhere up in the trees."

So she left the gnome
To go find herself
Somewhere out there
Between the northern lights
And the southern cross
Blithely fluttering about
Guided by a starry night
And Mother Nature's
Woodland trails.

ON MY OWN

If solitude
Is a safe haven
Then vulnerability
Is empowering beauty

NORTH

We only become more lost
When we drift
From the present moment.

May your North star,
Your heart's compass,
Bring you back
To the here and now.

No matter how far
You may wander
Or linger.

WILD SPIRIT

Live your life
In wide open spaces
Run wild
With nomadic free spirits
Smother the world
With your wanderlust kisses

24 HOURS

When you see
The sun and the moon
In the same waking,
That fleeting moment
With the bed unmade
Pondering the reality
You've lived
The past and present
On the same sweet day.

SWEET DARLING

Why are you in such a hurry, sweet darling?
If you don't know where you're going.

Let's linger
For a bit longer
Letting go
Of whatever it is
We're looking for.

STARTING OVER

Spread your wings
Dear sparrow
Take flight
To a happier tomorrow.

You can build a new nest
Wherever your heart lands
To rest,
To grow roots.

Beginning anew
Far, far away
From the traumatic abuse.

LUST

FITZROY

From up over
To down under
Her life in a backpack
The enigmatic Fitzroy
Is where she landed.

The first three months
A haze of yearning
For the man
Who lived in a loft
On Gore Street.

Complicated he was
Naive she were
Entangled in a romance
Both beautiful and bizarre
Destined to burst.

Then one Sunday morning
Over coffee and avo smash
At her favourite Min Lokal
The heart-confused lovers
Confessed they were over.

In the days after she would move out
Deciding her adventure in this sunburned country
Would not be about him
But about her own exploration
And falling in love with herself.

HAPPENSTANCE

Before you go
Before we go
Before we part ways
Say all the things

For we will never know
How we really felt
In this surreal moment
When me unexpectedly met

ECHOES OF THE IN-BETWEEN

In the space between
Is where you and I exist
The dreamscape where we first met
The haven where our broken promises are kept
The bed where you and I make love
Until we become no more
The dream distantly faded
Our hearts crumbled and jaded

In the present moment is where you and I
Is now just me and myself
The dreams are mine
The haven is my own heart
The bed is where I lay
The space is mine
For my self love to shine

TOMORROW'S LOVE AFFAIR

I did not know you yesterday
Yet here I am knowing
That I will fall in love with you
Tomorrow
And the days thereafter
Will be filled with nothing
But lustful sorrow

UNBROKEN RESOLVE

If pieces of me
Become pieces of you
How is it that my heart is whole
After the shattered mess you made
When you broke it
And left me behind
To clean up your adulterous mess

SPRING'S EMBRACE

In spring's horizon
Where cardinals fly
And songbirds sing
Where the morning wakes
To hues of fire lit kisses
That's where you will find me
Knotted up
In white linen sheets
Rising to your sweet smile
Our two naked bodies
Mine and yours
Wrapped up
In euphoric flaws so sweet
And our endless love
Eternally complete

PATHS APART

You went your way
And I went mine
I went blindly and broken
Into the night
Only to find
In the morning light
That I had left
Nothing behind

INDECISIONS AT MIDNIGHT

Daydreamers.
We have difficulty
Deciding where it is
And with whom we want to sleep.
It's why I lay awake at night
Wondering if the decision I made
To go home with you
After the whiskey and tequila
Was a good idea.
Even if you did feel so right
As we embraced
Beneath the howling moonlight.

LOST

May the wind blow
In whichever way
Your heart desires to go

TOMORROW'S PROMISE

And if met you tomorrow
Would you love me then
As much as you do today?

She quietly wondered
Her thoughts distracted
By his ravenous touch
As she let out a moan
Her pounding heart paused
And she realized it didn't matter
For this moment
Is where she wanted to stay

A KISS FULL OF LIES

Ladened with kisses
Sweet memories of you
Leave me stark naked
As you return to your mistress

GOOD SLEEPS

I yearn to share
Eternity with you,
Wrapped in our bed,
Enveloped completely
By the essence of us,
And the myriad hues
Of your tender kisses.

EMBRACE YOUR OWN STORY

Always remember
You are a stranger
Inspiring another person's story.
So, love yourself first and fiercely.
Make sweet love
To your own passionate protagonist.
Live every chapter without regret.
Turn the page
Enjoy the climax
But don't forget
Even if there is no happy ending
You loved bravely
Life is an adventure
There will be another stranger
Whose story you aren't a part of …
Yet.

LONELY

For all the restless nights
I stir awake by thoughts of you.
I sleep calmly
In the rare instance
When I get to lie next to you.

LOVE LETTER

You've given me a memory
That is as priceless
As a vintage stamp.
No return to sender
Just an everlasting image
Of you and I
That I might just mail
To myself
One day.

GHOSTED

I waited for you
Yes I did
But then you never came
So off I went

EPHEMERALITY

I was frozen in time until your lips kissed mine.
We stood still in an euphoric embrace.
I looked up at you nervously confused.
You smiled and said,
"This is the start of something special."
Then time resumed
And three months later
You kissed me for the last time.

FLEETING LUST

I ran wild
Emotionally free of you
Away from you
You were my tomorrow
Before yesterday even began
And when the sun settled
On our star-crossed love
You became my dearly departed

LETTING GO

The space between
Is where you will find me
I'm at peace to just be
Wherever you end up going
I hope your heart is happy
And no longer haunting
Me and my lovestricken dreams

WHISPERED NAMES

If I could hear your voice
Whisper my name
Then perhaps you could hear my heart
Screaming yours

A BEAUTIFUL CALAMITY

He had the most intriguing awkwardness
And she was a beautiful calamity
Two wanderlust lovers
With no rhyme or reason
For a happily ever after
But their hearts collide
And for a lustful season
They were in love
For a not so endless summer
Only for him to leave
And her to soon follow
But there on the corner
Of Smith and Gertrude Street
Their loved combusted
He left her
She stayed
Curious to see how life and love
Would endure as she moved forward

MELANCHOLY

NOTE TO SELF

Hungover and helpless
I picked myself up off the floor
Looking in the mirror
I heard myself say aloud:

Some of your days will be dark
And when they are remember
There is a beautiful horizon
Waiting for you
Beyond the silver lining
That's why we chase rainbows
On cloudy days

ABANDONED

Somewhere between here and there
I found you
But somewhere between then and now
I lost myself too

YESTERDAY'S LOVE

Blindsided
By bittersweet nostalgic of yesteryear
She did not recognize him
The man
Who she once loved
Strengthened by her sadness
She walked past him
In content silence
Looking over her shoulder
He smiled at her
And she waved goodbye
To a lifetime
Of melancholic memories

LUCKY NUMBER EIGHT

If we didn't fall apart at times
We'd never really see inside of ourselves.

A Japanese proverb tells us
'Fall down seven times
Get up eight'.

So, after you fall
Rest and repose
Let yourself heal.

For retrenching from life
Is necessary at times
How do we find peace otherwise?

Perhaps we find it
On the eighth try.

AND THERE YOU GO ... FINALLY

Ruminating memories
Faded into a broken recorded past
Who we were
Together
No longer matters
For I have forgotten you
Released and let go
At last

IN TRANSITION

In times of anguish
Of lost frustration
Remember always
That sadness
Is a transient emotion
A fleeting feeling
Brilliant, beautiful happiness
Will find you
Soon again

DEPRESSION

Here I stand
In the depths
Of mundane convention
Silently screaming in pain
For someone to rescue me
With divine intervention

BEAUTIFUL BRAVERY

Know that you can talk to me
Should you fear you will take your life
For no one should endure
Such lingering and lonesome
Sad, dark strife.

I am here for you
In any way I can
So, please don't give up, sweet darling
Give your heart - and life
Another chancE
To show your brave self
That you are worthy
Of this beautiful dance.

THE MORNING AFTER

The ashes of you
In my memory combust
As my heart burns
Up in flames.

The phoenix will not rise
For I am done with you ...
And the alcohol too.

ENDLESS SUNRISE

I found you yesterday
But you will meet her tomorrow
Today is all we have
To spend a lifetime together
So forgive me when I say
I hope the sun
Never sets

AN EMPTY PILLOW

And even though
I know
We are done
Forever
When I dream
There you are
Our love
Put back together
The morning after
With the window closed
And the stars gone
I rose to kiss you awake
But there beside me
You weren't anymore

LEFT HAND TURN

This is where
I leave you
And this is when
I find myself

BEAUTIFUL RUINS

Her heart is in pieces after he left her.
There she lies in imperfect, gorgeous ruins.
She will love again although differently than before.
Foolishly clumsy and ridiculously reckless
She was beautiful because she was broken.

SELF-WORTH REVELATION

I decided to leave you
When you stopped making me
Feel beautiful inside
You're not worth crying about
Over shattered pieces of a broken heart
No, you won't diminish
My self worth
Gratitude to you though
For your mean, abusive spirit
Turned my soul inside out
Inspiring me to look inward
And stand up for myself

RAIN TO SUNSHINE

I thought the tears falling
Were the mist from your eyes
But when I looked up
It was merely the rain falling
From the grey sky
When I blinked
My heart was basking
In sunshine

EXTINGUISHING EMBERS

A fairweather romance
Seldomly ignites
Into an ever after
Relentless desire
Destined to implode
A few moments of passion
Understood as infatuated lust

RESURGENCE

Replace anger
With acceptance
Replenish downheartedness
With hope
Accept that darkness will set
And morning light
Will rise tomorrow

OUR LAST NIGHT TOGETHER

With the window open
And the stars close
I rested in your arms
Falling asleep
To the beat of your heart.

We rose in bittersweet quiet
No words needed when we woke
For we knew what we had
Was a frugal love
Tired and broke.

That was the last night
We slept together
It was also the last time
We ever saw each other.

WEATHERED

You sweet and beautiful
Hypocritical mess
Seducing me
With that naked dress
Mad melancholy
Your mood suggests
A love scorned
Has left you
Weathered and depressed

BROKEN SHARDS

And she cried.
Not because she was alone
But because he had shattered
Her heart
Inside
Into a million pieces
Of broken shards of love.

And she was free.
To put her heart
Back together
Piece by piece
The perfect puzzle
To love her sweet self.

OUR LAST EMBRACE

Here I sit.
To breathe the last air of you
To taste the last kiss from you
To embrace the last hold from you
To give the last of my love to you.

Here I stand.
To explore the first day alone
With me and my heart
Bravely on my own.

Acknowledgements

My village is filled with the most supportive and encouraging humans. I could write an entire book acknowledging those that believe in me and fill my heart cup right full. Here are a few folks that I need to thank out loud - folks who unknowingly inspired me to turn my writing craft into a published anthology:

My dear girl, Shannon, whose authentic, artistic bravery gave me the courage and confidence to release my inner writer warrior.

My "Anam Caras" (soul friends), Sara and Mary, for their thoughtful birthday and holiday gifts of compilations by other poets and philosophers over the years. These gifts strengthened me and allowed me to share my words with the world.

My darling sisters, Melissa, Ashley and Felicia, my childhood friend Ang, my scrawesome bud Jason, and my German saint Kat who read every word and entertain my ramblings about dreaming of becoming a writer.

My Mama Bea for giving me roots and wings to fly ... and for knowing how influential spoken word artists like Leonard Cohen have been to me.

My tattoo artist, Nickola, who inked a quill pen on my right forearm saying, "to represent the writer that you are." Her words forever shaped the perception of my creative self.

My Aussie pals, Mat and Kel, for always asking me how my writing is going and reminding me to prioritize the craft that we love so much; a love that binds us.

My kindred spirit, Lee, for gifting me her talent and illustrating the images that accompany this collection of poems.

My husband, Dames, who built me a studio in our backyard so I have space to chronicle future chapters and finish my manuscript about my fictitious muse.

My community, for embracing me for who I am and for reading these words. I am forever grateful.

Mad love,
Nicxo

About the Writer

Nicole Beatty (aka NicBea) is a word artist, writer and wanderer. She has been archiving her journals since 1999, quietly nurturing her dream of one day becoming a published author. Nic's inspiration comes from her world travels, unrequited love, nature, community and other people's stories. She openly writes about her sobriety, struggles with infertility, her love for winter, and mental health.

Nic blogs at www.staticconfusion.com and she shares her writing on Instagram at @madlove_xx

About the Artist

Lee Higginson is an artist and photographer, with special interests in nature, upcycling and salvage art. Lee works primarily in community art facilitation with many organizations. She lives in Port Hope, Ontario, Canada with her two teenage sons.

You can find her online at @flukecraft

Copyright © 2024 by Nicole Elizabeth Beatty. All rights reserved.

This book, authored by NicBea of Cobourg, ON, Canada, is protected under the copyright laws of Canada and other countries. No part of this publication may be reproduced, distributed, or transmitted in any form or by any means, including photocopying, recording, or other electronic or mechanical methods, without the prior written permission of the publisher, except in the case of brief quotations embodied in critical reviews and certain other noncommercial uses permitted by copyright law.

Cover art and illustrations are copyrighted by Lee Higginson.

First printing, 2024.

www.ingramcontent.com/pod-product-compliance
Lightning Source LLC
Chambersburg PA
CBHW040748020526
44118CB00041B/2784